THE HOW AND WHY ACTIVITY WONDER® BOOK OF
CATS

Written by Sarina Simon
Illustrated by Lesley Boney

Reviewed and Endorsed by:

Georg Zappler
Publications Editor
Texas Memorial Museum
The University of Texas at Austin

Copyright © 1986 by RGA Publishing Group, Inc.
Illustrations Copyright © 1986 by Lesley Boney
Created by RGA Publishing Group
Published by Price/Stern/Sloan Publishers, Inc.
410 North La Cienega Boulevard, Los Angeles, California 90048

Printed in the United States of America. All rights reserved. No part of this publication may be reproduced, stored in a retrieval system, or transmitted, in any form or by any means, electronic, mechanical, photocopying, recording or otherwise, without the prior written permission of the publishers.

ISBN: 0-8431-4283-9

PRICE/STERN/SLOAN

Publishers, Inc., Los Angeles

1986

Introduction

The cat family is one of nature's largest families. It includes more than 33 kinds of wild cats like lions, tigers, leopards, and jaguars. It also includes the many different breeds of domestic cats that people keep as house pets.

Although they vary enormously in size, all cats, even house pets, belong to the same family. It is called *Felidae,* and it is divided into two branches. The larger cats, like tigers, lions and leopards belong to the *Panthera* branch. The smaller cats, like ocelots, bobcats, and domestic cats (which include Siamese, Persian and alley cats), belong to the *Felis* branch.

Many cats can purr, but some cannot. Can you guess which branch of the cat family is "purr-less"?

Family Ties

Even though they look very different from each other, all cats — from the mighty ten-foot tiger to the cuddly ten-inch kitten — have a lot in common. They are good leapers, springing on their targets from any position, almost flying through the air.

All cats are able to see very well in the dark. This is because they have a special lining in their eyes which can reflect light. In addition, their pupils are capable of opening very wide to let in any and all available light. All cats are carnivorous and have sharp teeth that cut and tear well. All except the cheetah have retractable claws. This means they can pull their claws back into their paws. When their claws are retracted they can creep about very quietly.

There are many sayings and myths about cats. One saying developed because cats hardly ever fall without landing on their feet.

To find out what the saying is, read the clues, unscramble these cat words and fill in the numbered blanks.

Clue	Scrambled	Blanks
What do cats walk on?	wspa	__ __ __ __ 1 2 3 4
How different are the sizes of cats?	yvre	__ __ __ __ 5 6 7 8
What is big and black and orange?	grite	__ __ __ __ __ 9 10 11 6 7
What can all cats do well?	plae	__ __ __ __ 12 6 2 1
What cat cannot retract its claws?	hhtecea	__ __ __ __ __ __ __ 13 14 6 6 9 2 14
What's a baby cat called?	niktet	__ __ __ __ __ __ 15 10 9 9 6 16

__ __ __ __   __ __ __ __   __ __ __ __   __ __ __ __ __
13 2 9 4   14 2 5 6   16 10 16 6   12 10 5 6 4

Do you think this saying is true?

Tigers

Tigers are the biggest cats in the world. Male tigers sometimes weigh as much as 600 pounds and grow to a length of 10 feet! Female tigers — tigresses — are smaller than males. They usually weigh about 300 pounds with an average length of eight to nine feet.

Tigers have extremely strong graceful bodies. They can jump 15 feet in the air or leap 10 yards barely making a sound. Their teeth are enormous and they can easily kill their victims with one bite. Most tigers have an orange-red to yellowish coat with black stripes. Their stripes make it easier for them to hide in the jungle bushes or tall grass.

The stripes on a tiger's face are like "fingerprints". No two tigers ever have the same stripe patterns.

Can you find this tiger's "faceprint" in the line-up below?

Siberian Tigers who live in snowy Siberia are the palest of all tigers. Can you guess why?

How Do Tigers Live?

Tigers are extremely adaptable and can survive in almost any climate as long as they have food, water, and a little shade. Many years ago they roamed in large numbers throughout Asia but today they are mostly found in India and Siberia with a few in China, Sumatra, and Java.

Although tigers are very quick and strong, they still have to work hard to get enough food for themselves to eat. Tigers are meat-eaters. They usually eat deer, antelope, and wild pigs. Most of the animals they hunt escape, and it sometimes takes weeks before they make a kill.

Tigers have huge appetites. They sometimes eat as much as 100 pounds of food at one time. That's about the same as 400 hamburgers!

Make your own picture of a tiger! Copy the lines inside the squares on the left into the same numbered squares on the right.

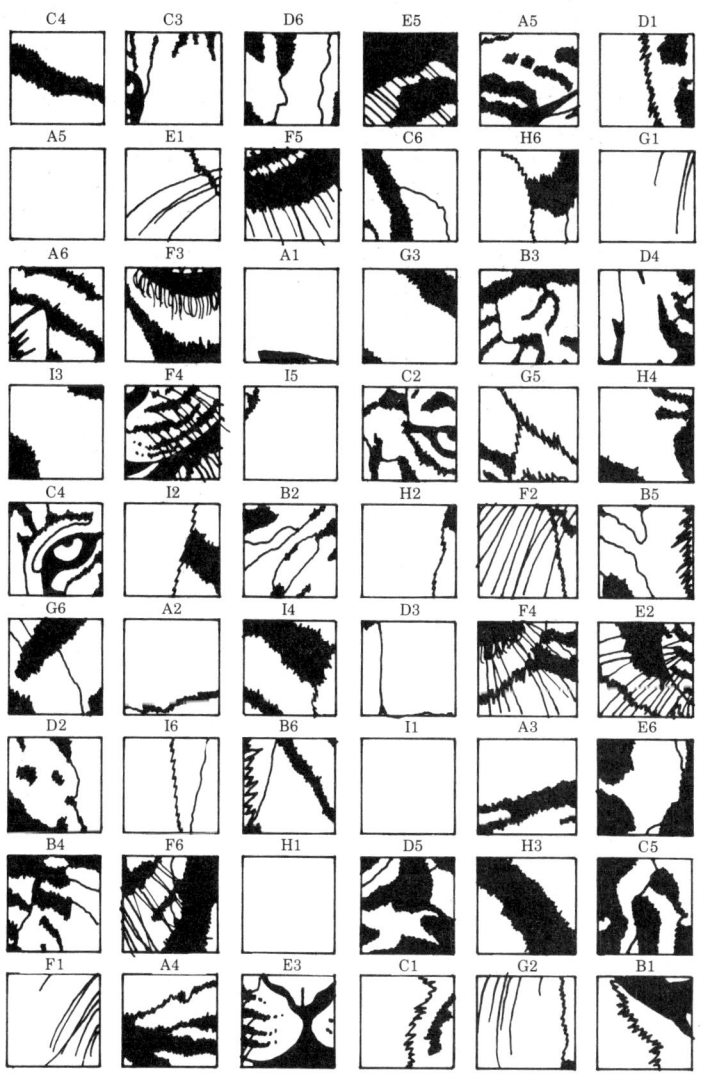

Cheetahs

Cheetahs are found on the plains and savannas of Africa and Asia. They weigh between 100 and 150 pounds and are about 4½ to 5 feet long. Cheetahs are the fastest land animals in the world. They can run faster than 70 miles per hour but only run for short distances. Cheetahs never run after an animal for more than 100 yards. If they cannot catch their prey in that distance, they hide in the bush and wait for another victim. Cheetahs usually hunt gazelles and springboks but they have also been known to attack flightless birds and baby zebras.

There are two kinds of animals that sometimes attack cheetahs to steal their food. Can you figure out what they are? Answer the questions, and fill in the numbered blanks.

Cheetahs usually hunt springboks and __ __ __ __ __ __ __ __
　　　　　　　　　　　　　　　　　　　　1 2 3 4 5 5 4 6

Cheetahs run faster than 70 miles per __ __ __ __
　　　　　　　　　　　　　　　　　　　　7 8 9 10

If cheetahs can't catch their prey, they hide in the bush and wait for another

__ __ __ __ __ __
11 12 13 14 12 15

Cheetahs live on the plains and __ __ __ __ __ __ __
　　　　　　　　　　　　　　　　　6 2 16 2 17 17 2 6

Cheetahs weigh between 100 and 150 __ __ __ __ __ __
　　　　　　　　　　　　　　　　　　　　18 8 9 17 20 6

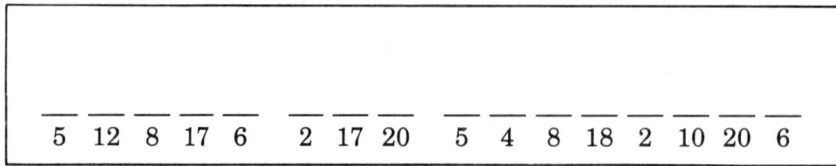

Tame Cheetahs

Cheetahs have a gentle disposition and can be tamed and put to work by people. In Iran, cheetahs are used by desert-dwellers as hunting "assistants". When they're not helping the adults to kill gazelles, they are playing like kittens with the village children. At one time, cheetahs were used by farmers in the United States to hunt and kill coyotes.

Although cheetahs can be helpful as hunters, they don't really make good house pets. They grow too large and need too much fresh food. Imagine feeding your pet cheetah a half a deer a day!

Cheetahs were kept as pets in ancient times but they were eventually replaced by an animal that was easier for man to care for. To find out the name of the animal circle the first letter in each answer word below:

1. A word that means the opposite of safe. _____

2. A word that means the opposite of young. _____

3. A word that means the opposite of bad. _____

4. A word that means the opposite of happy. _____

```
   __  __  __  __
   1.  2.  3.  4.
```

Leopards

Leopards are found in Asia and Africa. They are smaller than tigers but they are faster. They are very good climbers and can leap from limb to limb almost as well as monkeys do. Most leopards are between 3 and 5 feet long, weighing between 70 and 120 pounds.

The leopard is known for its secretive ways. It is shy, difficult to find, and difficult to see. It is hard to estimate how many leopards are left in the world since they are so good at staying away from people. Some leopards are yellowish with black spots. Others seem to be solid black but when they are examined closely spotted markings are visible. A female leopard can have yellow spotted and black kittens in the same litter.

Leopards have another name. To find out what it is, write the first letter of the name of each picture.

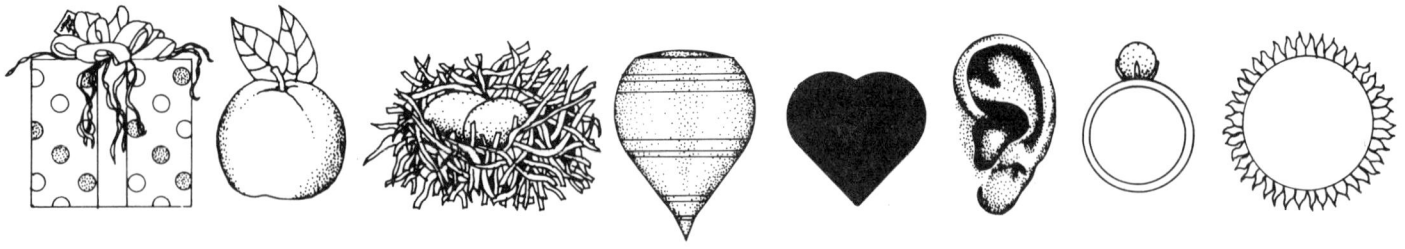

Leopards are also called _ _ _ _ _ _ _ _

8

How Do Leopards Hunt?

Leopards usually hunt at night. Most of the time they hide in the treetops and drop down on their prey. Their spots help conceal them among the branches as they wait for their victims. Occasionally, a leopard's long tail will hang beneath the branches and give away its hiding place.

Leopards kill their victims by strangling them with their strong jaws. They hardly ever eat their catch on the ground. Instead they drag it up into a tree where it will be safe from hungry hyenas and lions. Both spotted and black leopards have been known to kill human beings. Unlike tigers, who will only attack humans if the tigers are old or maimed, even strong, healthy leopards will attack a person.

You know all the words on this list. Can you find their proper places in the crosspatch? We've given you a head start.

Four Letters
Prey
Down
Time

Five Letters
Spots
Tiger
Their

Six Letters
Person
Branch
Beings

Seven Letters
Healthy
Leopard
Beneath

Bobcat

Bobcats are found in most of the United States, Southern Canada, and parts of Mexico. They can survive in a variety of environments and live in forests, swamps, deserts, and mountains.

Adult bobcats weigh between 15 and 30 pounds and are usually between 30 and 40 inches long. They are reddish brown in color with black and white tails. Bobcats eat rabbits, rodents, and birds. They tend to hunt at night and, like most other cats, they never kill more than they need.

Follow the directions below to solve this riddle.

QUESTION: What does a bobcat have in common with the wicked witch of the north?

S	X	W	Y	C	L	F	U
B	O	K	A	D	L	I	C
O	T	F	Z	U	Y	E	R

1. Cross out all vowels except the ones that rhyme with "bay" and "flea".
2. Cross out the consonants that are the initials of a fat jolly man in a red suit who works at Christmas time.
3. Cross out all the letters in the word, "flick".
4. Cross out all letters that come after W in the alphabet.
5. Cross out the second and fourth letters of the alphabet.
6. Use the remaining letters to write your answer below.

ANSWER: They both dislike __ __ __ __ __

Jaguar

Jaguars are found in the Southwestern United States, Mexico, Central America and many parts of South America. They live in many different habitats, including tropical jungles, mountains and desert-like plains. Jaguars are America's biggest cats — weighing anywhere from 150 to 300 pounds and growing to a length of five to six feet. Jaguars look a lot like leopards but a jaguar's rosettes often have black spots inside.

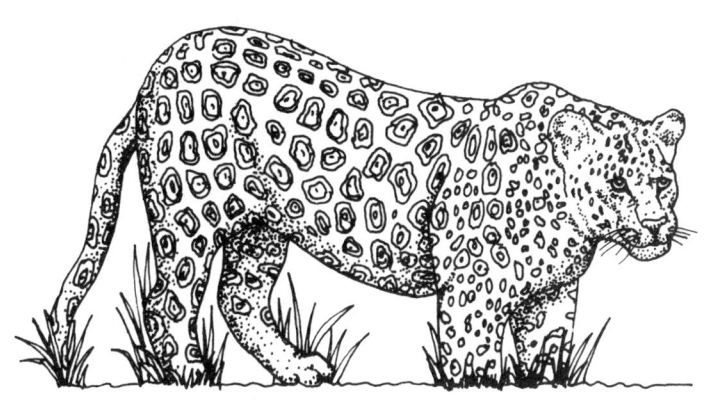

The jaguar was worshipped as a god in many ancient Latin American and South American civilizations. Many people felt that the jaguar was an animal by day and a "shaman" by night. To find out what "shaman" means, unscramble the words from the list at the right and fill in the numbered blanks. We've given you a head start!

Trosete $\underset{1}{R} \underset{2}{\_} \underset{3}{\_} \underset{4}{\_} \underset{5}{\_} \underset{5}{\_} \underset{4}{\_}$

Nutaiomns $\underset{19}{\_} \underset{2}{\_} \underset{6}{\_} \underset{7}{\_} \underset{5}{T} \underset{8}{\_} \underset{9}{\_} \underset{7}{\_} \underset{3}{\_}$

Ngrae $\underset{1}{\_} \underset{8}{\_} \underset{7}{\_} \underset{10}{G} \underset{4}{\_}$

Ustho $\underset{3}{\_} \underset{2}{O} \underset{6}{\_} \underset{5}{\_} \underset{11}{\_}$

Shaman means:

$\underset{19}{\_} \underset{4}{\_} \underset{18}{\_} \underset{9}{\_} \underset{12}{\_} \underset{9}{\_} \underset{7}{\_} \underset{4}{\_}$ $\underset{19}{\_} \underset{8}{\_} \underset{7}{\_}$

Acimear $\underset{8}{A} \underset{19}{\_} \underset{4}{\_} \underset{1}{\_} \underset{9}{\_} \underset{12}{\_} \underset{8}{A}$

Rujgaa $\underset{13}{J} \underset{8}{\_} \underset{10}{\_} \underset{6}{\_} \underset{8}{\_} \underset{1}{\_}$

Oicaltrp $\underset{5}{T} \underset{1}{\_} \underset{2}{\_} \underset{14}{\_} \underset{9}{\_} \underset{12}{\_} \underset{8}{\_} \underset{15}{\_}$

Igstbge $\underset{16}{\_} \underset{9}{\_} \underset{10}{G} \underset{10}{\_} \underset{4}{\_} \underset{3}{\_} \underset{5}{\_}$

Ofndu $\underset{17}{F} \underset{2}{\_} \underset{6}{\_} \underset{7}{\_} \underset{18}{\_}$

Many cars have been named after wild cats. How many can you think of?

How Do Jaguars Hunt?

Jaguars like the water more than most other cats. They are excellent swimmers and do not hesitate to chase a victim across a river or marsh. Jaguars eat peccaries, turtles, livestock, large fish, alligators, rodents and small animals.

Jaguars stalk their prey by crawling close enough to leap on their intended victim. In fact, the name jaguar comes from the South American word "jaguara" which means "meat-eater that overcomes prey in a single strike".

Make a jaguar puzzle! Color the picture first, then glue it onto a piece of cardboard. When it is dry, cut it into different shaped pieces. Mix up the pieces and try to put them back together again.

Mountain Lion

The mountain lion is the second biggest cat in America. It can be found in remote mountainous areas of the United States, Mexico and Western Canada. Mountain lions weigh anywhere between 147 and 227 pounds and grow to an average length of five to six feet. Mountain lions grow biggest where their favorite food — deer — is plentiful.

Mature mountain lions are covered with short yellow-brown or grayish hair. Cubs are a dusty gold color with black spots.

How many words can you make from the words, "Mountain Lion"? A score of 20 or more is excellent.

Are Mountain Lions Dangerous?

Mountain lions are among the shyest and most careful of all the cats. Although they generally avoid human beings, there have been a few reports of lions attacking people. In one case, the lion was protecting her kittens. In another, the lion attacked a man who was wearing a buckskin jacket. Experts believe that the lion may have mistaken him for a deer.

Mountain lions sometimes attack domestic livestock. For this reason, they are hunted by ranchers. Today, mountain lions are an endangered species. If the mountain lion is allowed to die out, the deer population will increase. Although this may seem like a good side-effect, the fact is that if the deer herds grow too large there will not be enough grass for them to eat. In the end, this will harm *all* the deer and the land itself!

There are five other names that are used for the mountain lion. Locate the letters in the box using the X Y coordinates to find out what they are.

```
   10 D R J I N E F W G H
    9 R E C B C D P V H L
    8 X Y Z A C T U O T G
    7 W C S O J I H G G R
X   6 Q B E L K U F F E A
    5 P M R X S B C T D S
    4 O L M I T O G L P T
    3 Z Q N M A P V A R V
    2 A P E O A Q X P E W
    1 L N O W V S T E R A
      1 2 3 4 5 6 7 8 9 10
              Y
```

X	Y		X	Y		X	Y	
9	7	=	9	7	=	9	3	=
3	8	=	2	5	=	2	1	=
1	2	=	4	4	=	5	8	=
5	8	=	1	2	=	2	5	=
10	10	=	5	8	=	5	2	=
6	3	=	2	9	=	7	4	=
7	10	=	1	9	=	6	6	=
						10	5	=
						8	9	=

X	Y		X	Y	
9	3	=	9	7	=
7	4	=	6	6	=
6	6	=	5	2	=
4	7	=	2	1	=
3	8	=			
1	9	=			

One of the mountain lion's names comes from the word "panther". Early American frontiersmen pronounced it wrong. Can you guess which name it is?

Lions

Lions are found in Africa on the grassy plains that border the jungles. The Asiatic lion, once widespread in southern Europe and the Middle East, can still be found in very small numbers in India. On the average, lions are a bit smaller than tigers. They usually weigh between 400 and 500 pounds and are about 6 to 7½-feet long. Most male lions have manes that cover their neck and shoulders. In zoos, these manes are full and thick. Out in the wild, they are shaggy and uneven because they get torn by thorns and bushes.

To find out what lion cubs look like when they are born, color in the spaces that contain words that relate to lions.

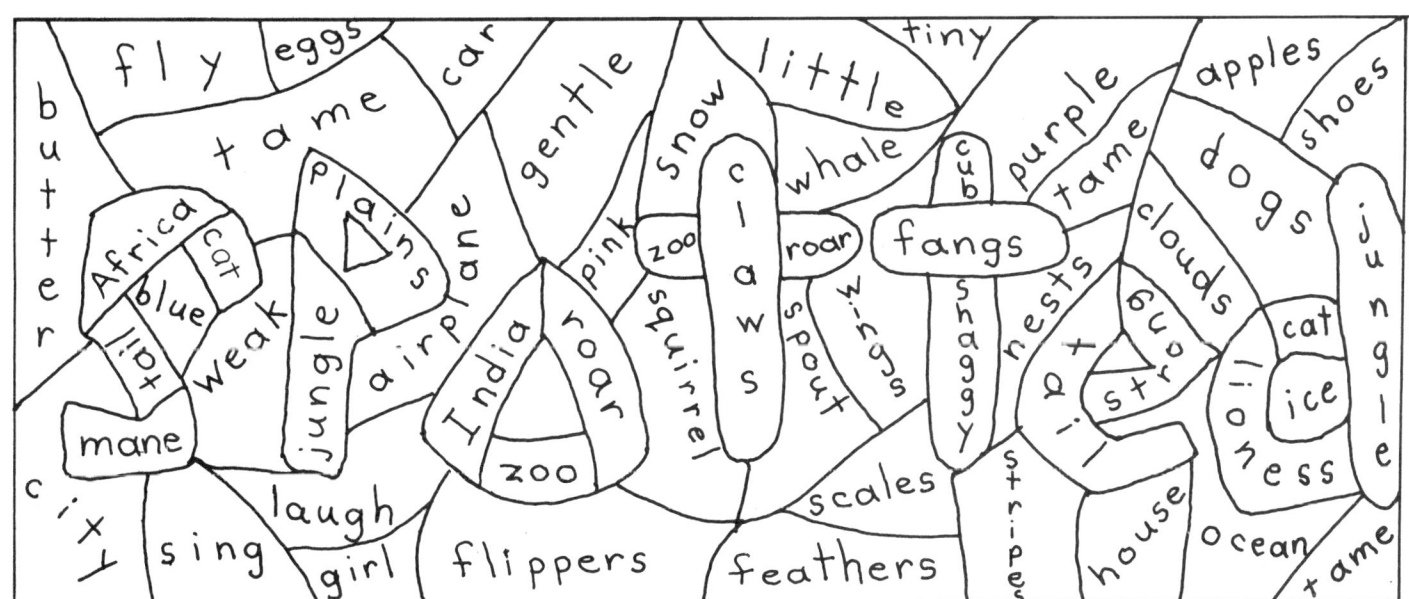

Lion cubs are born _____ .

15

Lion Families

Most lions live in *prides*. There are anywhere from four to forty lions in a pride. A pride usually has two adult female lions, all of their cubs under two years old and two adult male lions. Female lions remain in the same pride all their lives while males generally stay no longer than two years. Older males are usually driven out by younger, stronger males.

Every pride has its own territory. The territory is carefully guarded by the adult males. If a wandering adult lion happens into a pride's territory and meets another lion of the same sex, a fierce fight may break out. Sometimes, the "stranger" lion may kill an adult male and take over as leader of the pride.

However, a far worse enemy of the lion is man. Over the years thousands of lions have been killed by hunters and ranchers. Because of this, preservation laws have been created to protect this regal creature from extinction.

Some prides' territories are as small as ten square miles in area. Some are much bigger. Use the code to find out how big a pride's territory can be.

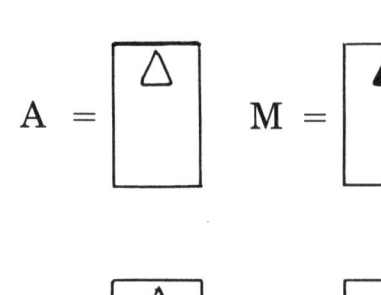

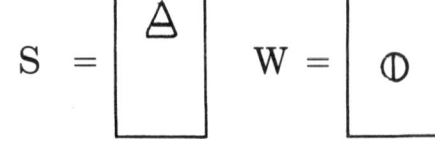

     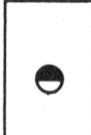 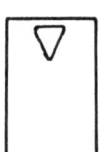   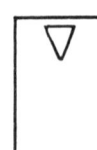

__ __ __ __   __ __ __ __ __

King of the Beasts

If a pride's territory has a lot of prey, lions do not have to work very hard. In fact, they generally spend about 20 hours a day sleeping or resting in the shade.

Male lions protect their pride and their territory but they hardly ever hunt.

Female lions do almost all the hunting. Females are better hunters than males since they are faster and can hide more easily.

Lionesses try to take their prey by surprise. This is important since many of their victims are a lot faster than they are. Lions prefer to eat buffalo, antelopes, giraffes, zebras and other smaller animals.

Complete the crossword by using the clues below.

ACROSS
4. The area where a pride lives.
10. Lions prefer to rest in the _____.
11. Lions usually do this once a day.
12. A very long period of time — rhymes with neon.
13. Something that is true.
14. Lions are a brownish-_____ color.

DOWN
1. A group of lions.
2. The opposite of stop.
3. A man-made waterway, the Suez _____.
4. Two times ten.
5. 2000 pounds.
6. 365 days.
7. Rock and _____.
8. The opposite of out.
9. You need one to open a lock.

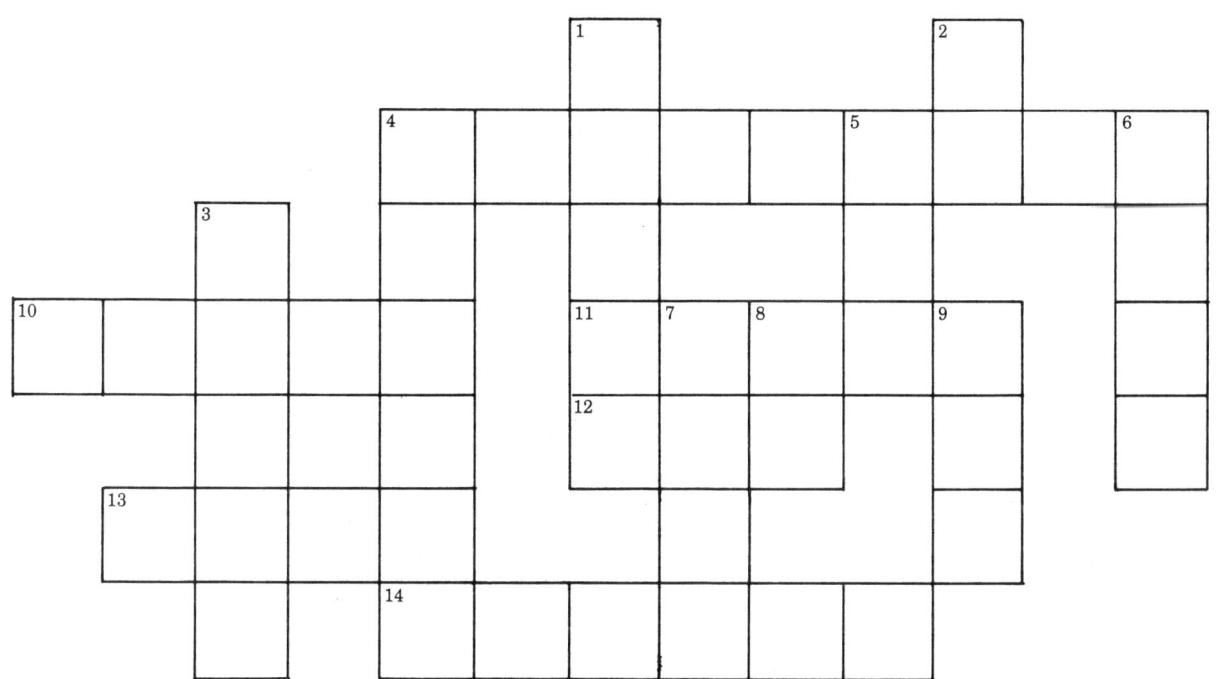

Ocelot

Ocelots are found in the forests and brushland of South America, Central America, Mexico, New Mexico, and Texas. They are medium-sized cats weighing between 25 and 35 pounds and growing to a length of 36 to 54 inches. Ocelots have beautiful coats. Their spots are orange-brown with black outlines. Their overall body color is a yellowish-gray. Ocelot furs are no longer allowed in the United States because the ocelot is an endangered species.

Ocelots hunt at night. They eat rodents, birds, fish, frogs, monkeys and other small animals. Ocelots usually hunt on the ground but they are very sure-footed and can easily stalk birds or monkeys in trees.

Some of the shapes on an ocelot's coat are more like odd-shaped blotches than spots. Cross out all the letters that appear four times or more to find out what the ocelot's spots are called.

A	J	V	H	X	P	V	C
F	R	B	O	V	C	B	F
S	H	E	P	J	T	C	P
F	H	B	A	H	P	F	A
F	T	J	E	X	V	C	X
B	V	P	X	F	S	A	J

They are called R O S E T T E S

18

Jungle Cat

The jungle cat is found in the woodlands and grassy areas of the Middle East and Asia. It usually weighs between 10 and 15 pounds and grows to a length of about 26 inches. The jungle cat is long-legged and its color varies from yellowish grey to reddish brown.

In ancient Egypt the jungle cat was tamed and trained to hunt birds. In fact, the jungle cat became the symbol of the goddess of the hunt, Bast. The Egyptians worshipped Bast in their temples and built statues in her honor. If you visit a museum with a good ancient Egyptian art collection you'll almost certainly find a statue of a jungle cat!

The ancient Egyptians loved their cats so much that they made them into something that would last forever. Use the clues to find out what they made.

1. The letter that is printed on a popular candy and is the 13th letter of the alphabet.
2. I love _____ ?
3. The first letter of the sound a cow makes.
4. The letter that you've already written twice in this puzzle.
5. The letter that would look like this 👁 in a rebus.
6. A letter that is in *pet* and *wet* but not in *tap*.
7. The curvy letter that sounds like the *C* in *ceiling*.

```
___ ___ ___ ___ ___ ___ ___
 1   2   3   4   5   6   7
```

Domestic Cats

Cats are among the most popular house pets in the world. In the United States alone there are more than thirty million! There are many different varieties of cats but they all fall into one of two groups — long-haired and short-haired. Their colors can vary from black, yellow, orange, silver and tortoise-shell, to white and even blue.

Unlike dogs, cats are very independent. One minute they are snuggling on their owner's lap and the next, they are leaping off in pursuit of a bird or a ball of yarn.

Cats seem to get great satisfaction from washing and grooming themselves. Using their tongues and front paws, they begin with the face and finish with the body. Because a cat's tongue is so rough, it can clean the dust and dirt from its fur.

Cats still have their hunting instincts and, if necessary, can survive in the wild. In fact, cats have been known to return to the wild and do quite well. In one case, a fully grown cat returned to the wild and doubled both his weight and size. When a domestic cat returns to the wild in this way it is called a *feral* cat.

All cats, even wild cats, are thought to be descended from an animal that lived 40 million years ago. This is its picture.

To find out its name, write the first letter of the name of each picture.

It is called _ _ _ _ _ _ _ _

Rex Cats

Rex cats are easy to recognize because of their curly fur. Their coats resemble poodle fur. Even their whiskers are curly. Oddly enough, the first rex cat was born into a litter of straight-haired cats in 1950. It was the only kitten with curly fur and so it was called a mutation. The owner, a Cornish farmer in England, raised rex rabbits so he gave the unusual kitten the name of rex cat. After this, the kittens of this particular cat were known as Cornish rex cats.

A few years later another mutation happened in Devon, England. This curly rex cat was called a Devon rex. Even though both rex cats are curly furred the two types are unrelated. When a Cornish rex cat mates with a Devon rex, amazingly enough, their kittens are all straight-haired!

The rex cats can be bred to have any color coat. They are very hardy cats that love to romp and climb.

This rex cat wants to climb. Help him find his way to the tree:

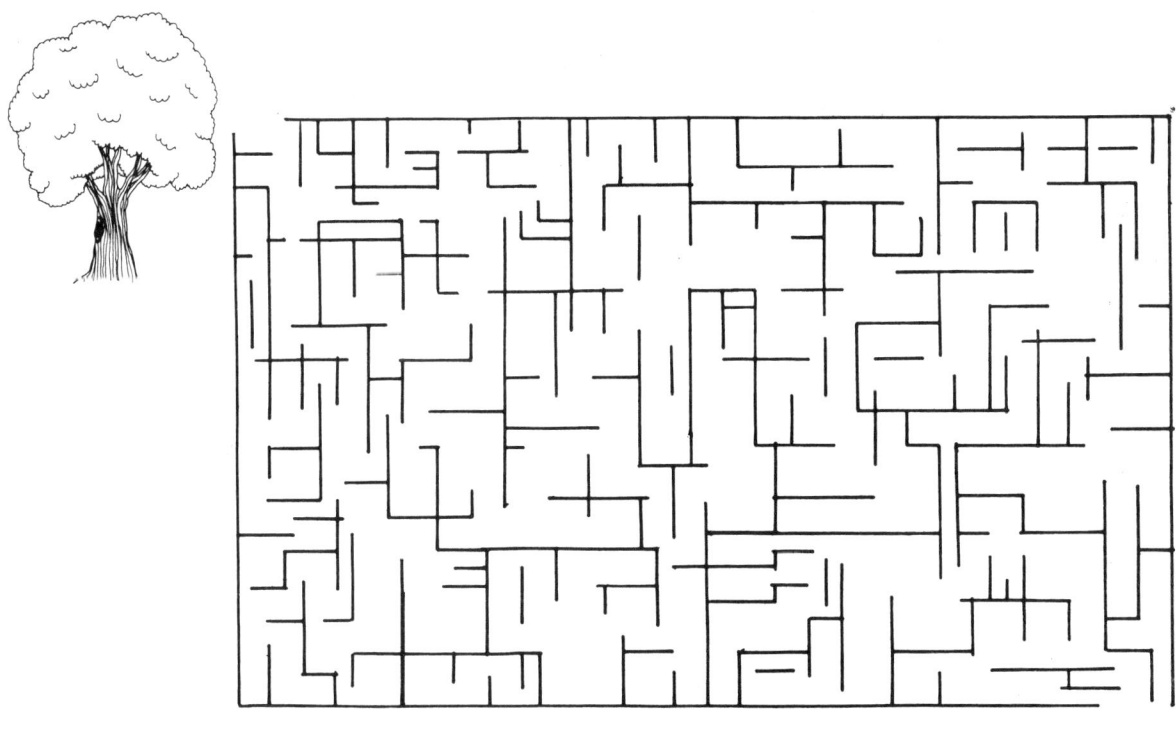

Siamese Cats

Siamese cats are probably the most popular breed of cats in the world. They originally come from Siam (called Thailand, today) where they were considered by some priests to be sacred. Siamese cats arrived in America by ship in the California gold rush days.

There are many varieties of Siamese cats. All of them are short-haired and dainty with slanted blue eyes. One of the most loved varieties is the seal-point Siamese.

Seal-point Siamese kittens are born with white fur. When they are a few months old most of their fur changes to a pale cream color. Other Siamese cats have body colors ranging from white to ivory to light brown. All Siamese cats have "points" of darker fur on their faces, tails, feet, legs and ears.

Complete the crossword by using the clues below

ACROSS
1. Religious leaders.
2. What a ghost says.
3. What you write when you want to add more to a letter.
4. Members of the Felidae Family.
5. The U.S. flag is red, white and _____.
6. To go away or exit.
7. Her, she. My, _____.
12. It sounds just like sew.
14. Someone who presses a doorbell.

DOWN
1. Well-liked.
5. A particular type of animal.
8. The opposite of out.
9. Cats with slanted eyes.
10. A signal for help.
11. We can _____ with our own eyes.
13. A word that sounds like oar.

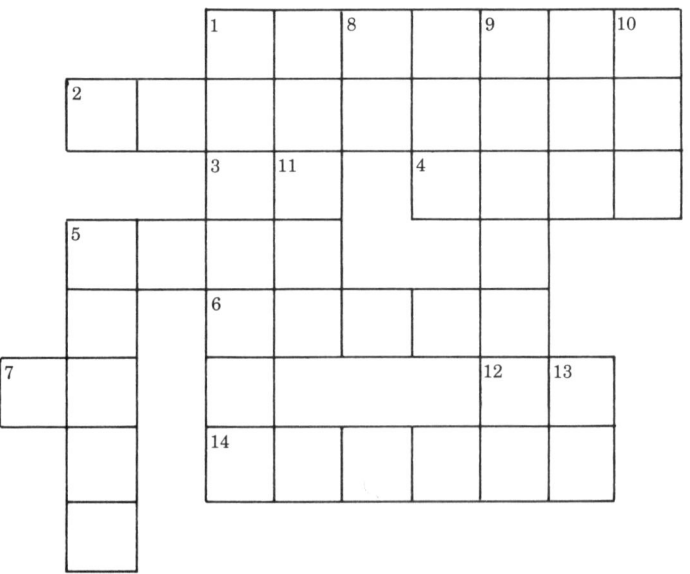

The Manx

The Manx is a short-haired cat with a very unusual characteristic — it has no tail! Most people believe that it developed as a mutant from ordinary cats living on the Isle of Man in the Irish Sea. The Manx is a very good hunter and is a popular mouse catcher on English and American farms. Its excellent hunting abilities may have something to do with its extraordinary speed — the Manx can run as fast as 30 miles an hour! A Manx may be almost any cat color. Its head is round and its cheeks are wide and somewhat pointed. The hind legs of a Manx are considerably longer than it's front legs, and the Manx sometimes hops like a rabbit.

Like all cats, including its distant cousin the tiger, the female Manx is a very good mother, and teaches her kittens how to take care of themselves.

Use the code to find out what book the Manx is reading.

A	//	G	□	M	※	S	=	Y	◻
B	⬡	H	×	N	⊙	T	‖	Z	⏇
C	⚲	I	D	O	⌀	U	⊙		
D	ϙ	J	ᴜ	P	−	V	⌽		
E	⚥	K	ꓷ	Q	+	W	◑		
F	♀	L	⌒	R	\\	X	⊘		

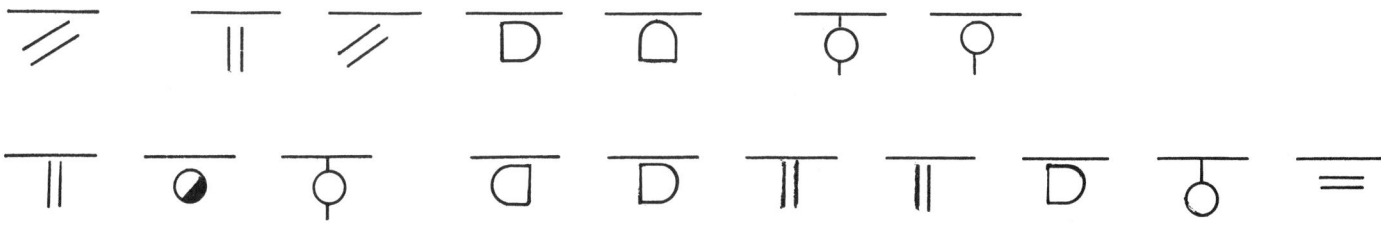

Do you know what "people" book has a similar title?

Persian Cats

The Persian, like all long-haired cats, comes from Central Asia. A native wild cat, called the Pallas cat, which lives in snowy areas and has long hair, is believed to have interbred with the Egyptian domestic cat. This brought about the Persian variety.

Persians are often considered "show" cats more than household pets. This is probably because they are so beautiful and they are less playful than most cats. Persians have full bodies with short legs. They have tiny noses and round eyes that may be orange, copper, yellow, blue or green. Their long-haired coats are very silky and vary in color from white to black.

See how many words you can make from "Persian Cat". If you find 35 words or more your score is excellent.

Calico Cats

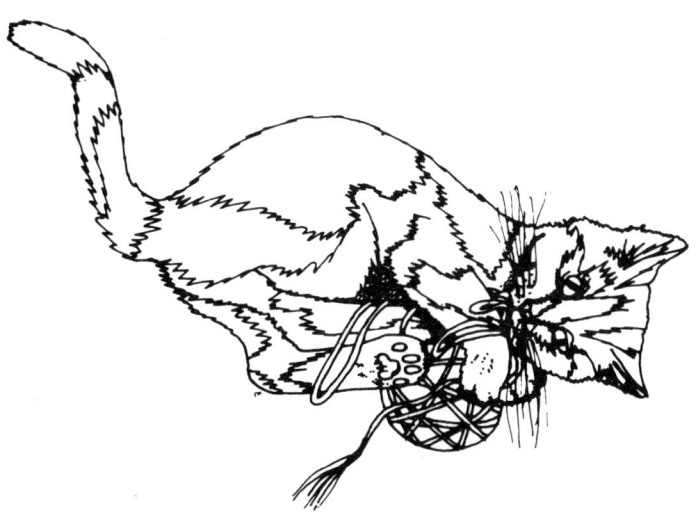

The four-colored calico cat is an adorable animal with a coat that resembles a patchwork quilt made up of black, cream, orange and white short-haired or long-haired fur. It has a small face and a nose that is half orange and half black.

Calicos are usually born to mothers who have tortoise-shell colored coats. Like leopards, who can have spotted and black cubs in the same litter, calico cats can have tortoise-shell and calico kittens in the same litter.

Like all domestic cats, calicos tend to rest in the daytime and prowl at night. Like their distant relative, the lion, domestic cats spend almost $2/3$ of their day sleeping!

This Calico cat has been prowling all night. Help him find his way home again.

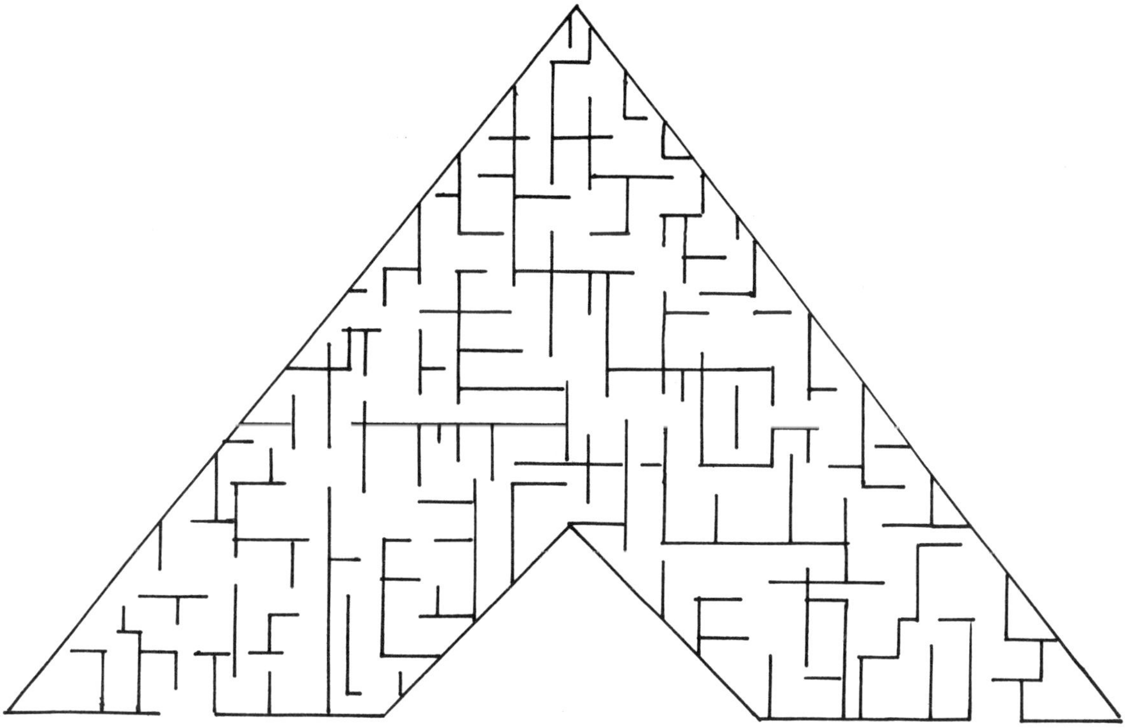

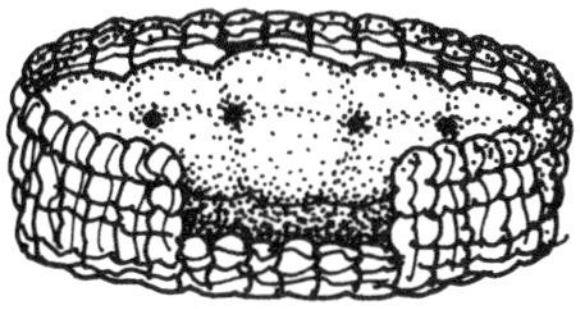

Tabby Tigers and Russian Blue Cats

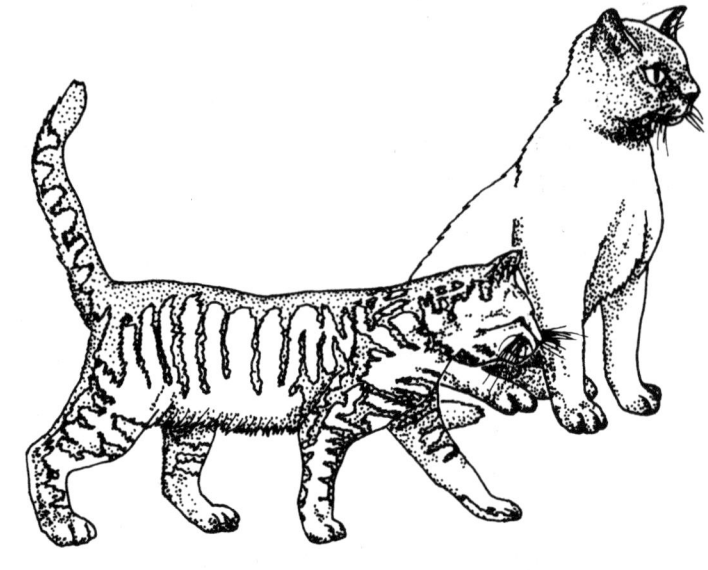

The tabby tiger and the Russian blue are both short-haired cats. The tabby tiger is the most common domestic cat in the United States and England; while the Russian blue is most popular in Northern Russia, Sweden, Finland, Poland, Germany and Denmark.

Tabby tigers come in many different colors, usually with blackish markings that make them look almost striped. Tabbies get their name from "Atabi" silk, which their coats are said to resemble.

The Russian blue cat is one of the few cats that walks along happily on a leash. Although it is called a blue cat, it is actually a slate gray or lilac color. Russian blues are popular stars in cat shows throughout Europe.

Pretend that you are a Russian blue or a tabby tiger. Write a letter to your pen pal. If you are a Russian blue, write to a tabby tiger in Florida. If you are a tabby, write to a Russian blue in Siberia.

Dear _____ ,

   I'm sorry I haven't written sooner. The weather has been _____. Every day it _____ and I have to wear my _____ to go outside.

   My owners are angry with me because I _____ last night. I couldn't help it, I wanted to _____.

   I have found that I love to eat _____. It's very easy to get here in _____ because it is found in the _____. Have you ever tried it? I hope someday we'll get a chance to meet.

Your friend,

_____

The Abyssinian

One of the oldest breeds of cats is the Abyssinian. In fact, Abyssinians look very much like the statues of sacred cats that were worshipped in ancient Egypt. They have long slender bodies and are extremely acrobatic. They are one of the few cats that enjoy swimming and were once trained to catch water birds.

Their short fur has an unusual marking called ticking. Every hair has two or three bands of color, ranging from reddish brown to grey or black. This ticking gives the Abyssinians a jungle appearance. Even though they look quite a bit like their cousin, the lion, Abyssinian cats are among the gentlest and friendliest of the domestic cats.

Their eyes are yellow, green or hazel and their large ears are pricked up in such a way as to make them seem to be listening. They are known to be very intelligent and loyal cats.

Find the words that describe the Abyssinian cat. Circle as many as you can. Some words go across, some down.

P	L	I	S	T	E	N	I	N	G	P	Y	S
O	I	E	L	S	W	S	L	E	N	D	E	R
F	R	I	E	N	D	L	Y	T	I	N	L	E
U	N	L	Z	E	O	A	G	H	K	T	L	M
B	H	I	A	E	G	Y	P	T	C	D	O	M
E	J	O	H	R	I	O	T	J	I	P	W	I
G	T	N	E	G	I	L	L	E	T	N	I	W
C	I	T	S	E	M	O	D	A	N	N	L	S

Slender
Intelligent
Ticking
Swimmers
Loyal
Domestic
Lion
Egypt
Hazel
Yellow

The Maine Coon Cat

The Maine coon cat got its unusual name from New Englanders who thought it was a cross between a raccoon and a cat. With the dark rings on its tail and black "mask" stretched from eye to eye it does indeed look like a raccoon. However, its ancestors were all cats. It is thought to be a descendant of the Angora cat; a relative of the Persian cat that was brought to America by early settlers.

The Maine coon cat is quite large and muscular. The males can weigh as much as forty pounds and the females more than twenty pounds. They have long fur that varies in color and markings. These cats are unusual in that sometimes they have extra toes on their forepaws and hindpaws. This condition is called polydactylism (poly-DAK-ti-lism). These extra toes make their feet broader, almost like snowshoes. Because of this, they move quite easily across winter snow.

Some New Englanders say that these intelligent cats are good weather predictors.

An old saying claims that, "If a coon cat scratches a fence one day, it will surely ____ ___ ____ !"

Use the clues to find the answer

1. The letter at the end of the sound a happy cat makes.
2. A good grade on a school paper.
3. A letter that sounds like a part of your face.
4. The first letter in a word that means the opposite of day.
5. The fifth letter in the name of a country where cats were worshipped.
6. The first letter in the word that means the opposite of cold.
7. The vowel in both "hazel" and "green".
8. The last letter of the name of a distant relative of the coon cat.
9. The first letter in the name of a large animal with a trunk.
10. The twenty-fourth letter of the alphabet.
11. The first letter of three of the numbers between 1 and 11.

Looking Back

There is something wrong in each of these pictures. Using the information you learned in this book, tell what is wrong with each picture.

Answers

PAGE 2
The Panthera branch is "purr-less".

PAGE 3
Paws, Very, Tiger, Leap, Cheetah, Kitten.
Cats have nine lives.

PAGE 4
The tiger on the top, right is the same.

PAGE 5

PAGE 6
Gazelles, Hour, Victim, Savannas, Pounds
Lions and Leopards

PAGE 7
Dangerous, Old, Good, Sad = Dogs

PAGE 8
Present, Apple, Nest, Top, Heart, Ear, Ring, Sun = Panthers

PAGE 9

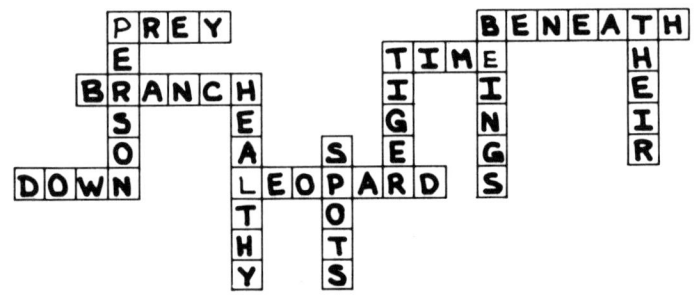

PAGE 10
Water

PAGE 11
Rosette, Mountains, Range, South, America, Jaguar, Tropical, Biggest, Found = Medicine Man

PAGE 13
Mount, main, maul, malt, mint, out, oat, on, nun, nut, no, not, noun, ton, tail, tin, tuna, ant, aunt, in, inn, into, it, ion, no, noun, not, lit, lint, _____ ?

PAGE 14
Cougar, Painter, Puma, Panther, Catamount

PAGE 15
Spotted

PAGE 16
One hundred square miles!

PAGE 17
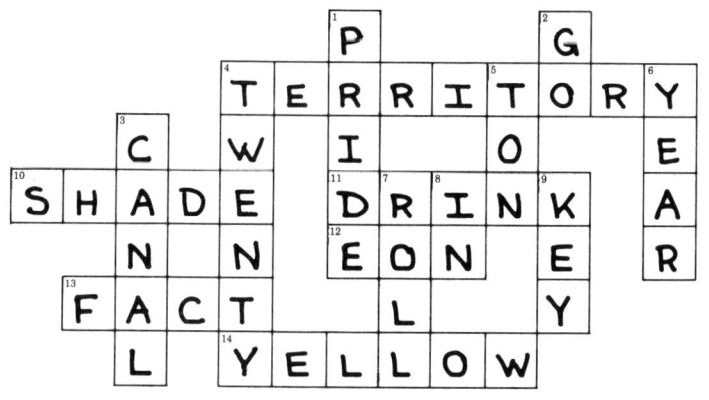

PAGE 18
Rosettes

PAGE 19
Mummies

PAGE 20
Dinictis

PAGE 21
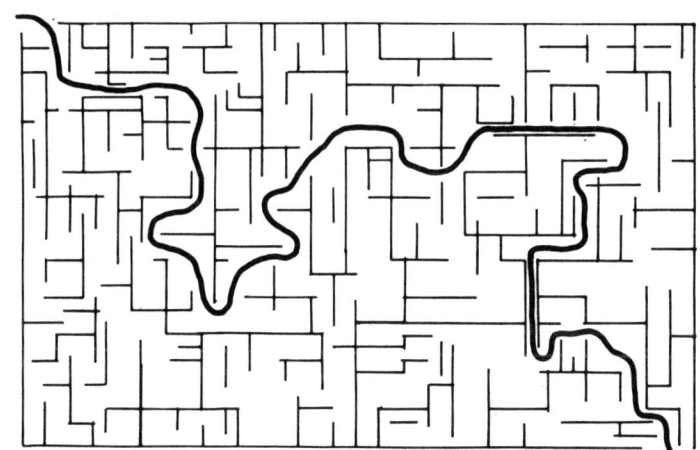

PAGE 22
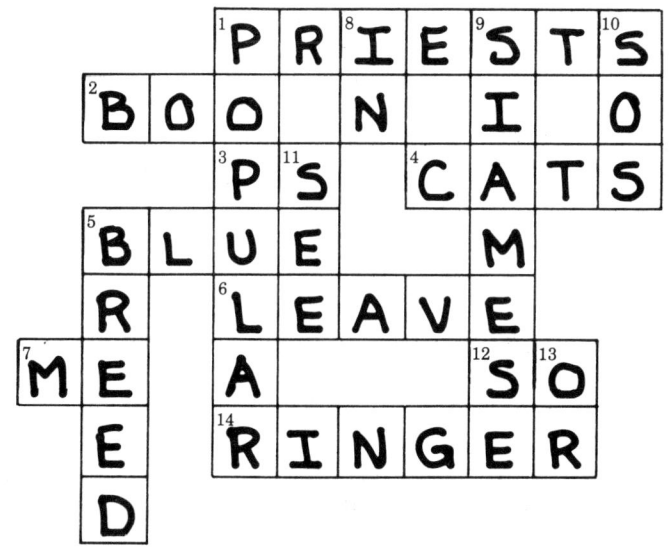

PAGE 23
A tail of two kitties

PAGE 24
Pan, pin, pat, eat, rip, rat, ran, sir, sit, sip, sat, seat, sear, sap, scan, scat, in, it, ire, as, an, ape, at, ate, art, arc, are, ant, nest, nip, near, can, car, carpet, tin, tan, tap, tiara, tar, tarp, _____ ?

PAGE 28
Rain the next!

PAGE 29
1. Tigers are meat-eaters, 2. Manx cats don't have tails, 3. Tigers are bigger than lions, 4. Cheetahs are faster than lions, 5. Cheetahs don't make good pets, 6. The Egyptians worshipped cats, not dogs.

PAGE 25

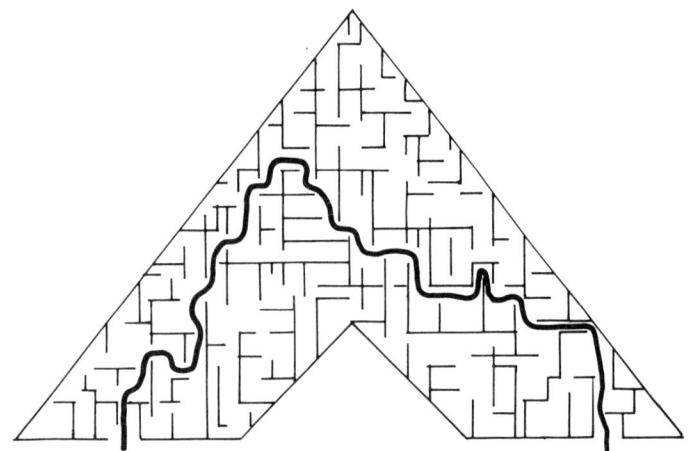

PAGE 27